MADMAN AT KILIFI

African
POETRY
BOOK SERIES

Kwame Dawes, editor

MADMAN AT KILIFI

Clifton Gachagua

Foreword by Kwame Dawes

University of Nebraska Press / Lincoln

"At the Suicide Galleria" and "A Genre
of Isolation" were first published in
Saraba magazine. "Ghostwriter" was an
advert posted on the oDesk website.

This volume is published in association
with the African Poetry Book Fund.

Library of Congress Cataloging-
in-Publication Data
Gachagua, Clifton, author.
Madman at Kilifi / Clifton Gachagua;
foreword by Kwame Dawes.
pages cm.—(African poetry book series)
Poems.
ISBN 978-0-8032-4962-2 (pbk.: alk. paper)
ISBN 978-0-8032-5443-5 (pdf)
ISBN 978-0-8032-5444-2 (epub)
ISBN 978-0-8032-5445-9 (mobi)
I. Dawes, Kwame Senu Neville, 1962–
writer of introduction. II. Title. III.
Series: African poetry book series.
PR9381.9.G226M33 2014
821.92—dc23   2013028621

Set in Garamond Premier by Laura Wellington.

To Eunice Njambi Mbugua

and my mother, Susan Njeri

CONTENTS

The Kenya of Clifton Gachagua is cosmopolitan. It is a world of cyber-communication, of cultures intersecting with each other, of existentialist angst, of faiths, of multiple languages, of a swirl of ideas and anxieties, of political intrigue and boredom. It is a world of youthful abandon, of passion, of sexual ambivalence and willful ambiguity; it is a world in which a sensitive, whimsical, sardonic, and intelligent poet walks through and observes in ways that leave us breathless with the freshness of what he sees and how he feels.In many ways, what we find in Gachagua is a poet's articulation of the complexities of traditional culture and ultramodern realities that exist sometimes comfortably with each other and at times in deep conflict on the continent of Africa.

But this is about all one can say in general terms about Gachagua as an African poet. The problem is, of course, the fact that Africa is such a large and varied continent, and yet it has been one of those places that has repeatedly been defined in totalizing and collective terms. Indeed, more often than I care to remember, I have heard people speak of the continent as if it is a country. And yet, one of the challenges of this new initiative for African poetry is the way in which collectively, African poetry has not had the kind of access to publication as one would imagine it would, whether at the level of individual nations or on the continental level.

It would be fascinating to try to arrive at some of the reasons why this is the case, but that is not my task here. My task here is to say that Gachagua's poetry represents a clear indication of what this state of affairs is: a travesty and most unfortunate.

Madman at Kilifi offers us ample evidence that the remarkable changes that are taking place in Africa today are ripe for the poet's imagination. Gachagua's poems reveal the speaker's sense of uncertainty in a society that is still trying to redefine its ideas of democracy in ways that are reflective of the peculiar history of that nation. He writes his poems no longer from the position of a person inscribed in the British colonial presence, but from that of a man fully consumed by, and in lively contention and engagement with, American cultural imperialism through films, television, music, and technology and its political power. Whereas the postcolonial writers of a couple of generations before Gachagua might have seen themselves largely writing against the colonial legacy of the British, Gachagua has the seemingly more complex dilemma of addressing the ubiquitous presence of American culture in Kenyan society—a culture, that, unlike the British imperialist presence, seemingly has a place for Africa in its very conception. Hip-hop music, the civil rights movement, Motown, and the power of African American culture complicate the way that Africa apprehends America. In many ways, rejection of American imperialism cannot be thorough or absolute, nor is it fraught with the same kind of Fanonesque psychological trauma that may have operated in the postcolonial narrative.

Gachagua has found in the largely eclectic nature of American poetic aesthetic a working model for his own work, which is best read in the tradition of "road" poetry—poetry that seeks to capture the varied and unpredictable world that a poet sees on the road. One thinks of movement when one thinks of Gachagua's poetry, movement across the state of Kenya and beyond to other parts of Africa. His speaker is an unwilling prophetic figure walking the streets of his cities, seeing things, and in the process naming things afresh. And it is this effort that one finds to be of greatest value to readers. Gachagua is not a guide. He is not introducing us to his world. He is simply seeing the world as if he is guiding himself through it. Kamau Brathwaite's naming of Barbados in his long poems *Sun Poem* and *Mother Poem*, or Derek Walcott in his epic *Another Life*, or Lorna Goodison in her resurrecting of the voices and places of Jamaica in her collection *Golden Grove*, or Kerouac in his work *On the Road*, or HD in her effort to make sense of London during the war years in *Trilogy*, or Whitman in *Leaves of Grass*—all these men and women assuming the audacity of a kind of Adamic function of naming things are, indeed, trying to make sense of their often uncharted worlds, and to do so with a lyric, poetic impulse.

This is where the urgency lies in Gachagua's work. The urgency is to capture the world before it disappears. And the urgency is further realized in the fact that in his effort to understand this world he is, in fact, trying to understand himself. This sense of movement is one we are alerted to very early in the collection. "A Slow Boat to China" offers, in one instance, something of an overture for the entire collection. The themes will be echoed and reechoed throughout. I will do something unusual as a way to introduce Gachagua's superior instincts as a poet—one single example, examined closely, as a way of showing us something of what Gachagua has achieved in this collection:

The trip begins in a landlocked country with a navy and old sea captains,
geologists and dark men who speak quick Arabic.
Where is she? On a slow boat to China with her braids floating
on salt water. The country used to have a port before secession.
Next to her is a man who either carries all his money in a leather pouch
or keeps it buried at home.
The import/export business is booming, maritime is a beautiful word
when the Indian Ocean is all you have between you
and a promised land.
They are heading to a small town on the coast,
with a name as obscure as a footnote in a Britannica,
to buy polythene bags and goods in high demand.
He quotes Brutus and kisses her ankles,
leaving a trace of henna from his quick mouth.

First of all, we have to accept that we may never be entirely sure of Gachagua's geography. The poem begins in a landlocked country that Kenya is not, but it is a country where sea captains and a navy exist. It is also a place where Arabic is spoken. A woman makes an appearance in this poem, and she (or some version of her) will reappear in a significant proportion of the poems. Often the poems are not casually engaged with who she is, but equally as often she is like us, an observer, there for the ride. The speaker is speaking love poems throughout the collection, and yet the "love" is incidental. The landlocked country once had its own port, but the political turmoil of Africa has led to it no longer having a port. We move from politics to the economics of exploitation and boom dynamics: "The import/export business is booming, maritime is a beautiful word." The characters in the poem are heading to a town with an obscure name (one that is described as a "footnote in "Britannica"—a stand-in, no doubt, for the colonial legacy of the past) to purchase bags and goods to sell. They are involved in that booming business. But Gachagua takes us no further. He observes the world and then leaves it for the distraction of troubled love—the "Brutus kiss" and the henna, allusions that point to Western traditions and Eastern traditions at one time. Gachagua's Kenya is a place of roads that cross, of seaports, of ships that enter and leave bringing goods and cultures into the complex world of coastal east Africa—a world that has been cosmopolitan for centuries and centuries.

Gachagua's poems are urgently present; they emerge out of sources like the radio, newspaper, television, as well as street stories and rumors. They seek to chart a changing society and while the effort is largely impossible to accomplish, the gesture is important. One of Gachagua's whimsical speakers describes himself as a "cartographer of water," and in this Gachagua seems to have found the fit metaphor for his art—quixotic, absurd, and yet necessary. To do this, Gachagua is unabashed about exploring themes of death, sexual adventure, violence, betrayal, and those things that some might term deviant in his poems. The result is a book that is arresting and full of surprises. Fortunately, this material is being handled by a craftsman who has clearly given much of his apprenticeship to the study of both contemporary and past poets. What is most appealing about Gachagua, however, is even though you can tell that he has read his fill of Shakespeare, Eliot, and Ginsberg, one has the sense that he is not shackled by them but is willing to bend them to his purposes.

The judges of the inaugural Sillerman First Book Prize for African Poets have agreed that without a doubt, we are experiencing in this book the opening noises of a poet who will make a great deal of important noise in the future.

MADMAN AT KILIFI

Charcoal on Canvas

Charcoal on canvas #2
is the name you give me as a substitute
for the times you deny me the luxury
of eating berries off your belly button.
You are afraid the mint liquor will seep under your skin
and make your nipples ripe with grief
and the heavy intonations of my nighttime monologues

A Slow Boat to China

The trip begins in a landlocked country with a navy and old sea captains,
geologists and dark men who speak quick Arabic.
Where is she? On a slow boat to China with her braids floating
on saltwater. The country used to have a port before secession.
Next to her is a man who either carries all his money in a leather pouch
or keeps it buried at home.
The import/export business is booming, maritime is a beautiful word
when the Indian Ocean is all you have between you
and a promised land.
They are heading to a small town on the coast,
with a name as obscure as a footnote in a *Britannica*,
to buy polythene bags and goods in high demand.
He quotes Brutus and kisses her ankles,
leaving a trace of henna from his quick mouth.

Satellite

They spoke with satellite mouths and gathered words between
their phalanges like hands in sacks of rice
throwing them to us, offering them to us as we slept. But we
were really going down the aisles with a
common veil around our misery like a good dream hanging
above our black and silver faces. They were beautiful and we
were beautiful before that. Beauty was a long marathon and a
blind man waiting
at the finish line, with silver bronze gold amulets for each and
every one of us despite the position at the podium.
We were aware of their hands above us as we slept. We woke up
tired, our mouths tired, our language tied.
We posed in our sleep because they were taking pictures from
small passages in their palms.
Their bodies were singing machines. They gave birth and were
born from old grandfather clocks.
Each pore in their body was a pinhole and the slightest muscle
movement led to a billion photographs
culminating in the blood. This is how memory worked for
them. They hadn't seen such beautiful sleeping bodies. They
wanted our photographs to take in our sleep, unethical
where we were dreaming of a shifting finish line. Beauty was
a thing you could savor with your tongue sticking out like a
reptile.
Pass on to the stranger sitting next to you in the bus through
the umbilical.
It was there in the air, exacting a gravitational pull on us,
keeping us stuck to the ground. The most we could do
was collide against each other. Light was graceful to the places
below the epidermis and we glowed like undiscovered galaxies
and shifting matter.

At the Confucius Center

All he could do was quote the great philosophers of our time;
Zizek and some other obscure men from the motherland
who praise violence as virtue, dissidents
who spent their exile years smoking cigarettes and
brewing coffee in small rented apartments.
He forgot how to talk. What he did was quote
coded passages from the postmodernists.
He fell in love with violence in books,
and the slapstick humor of crooks in Quentin Tarantino films.
He maintained an e-mail relationship with a gay pacifist
and second-year law student from Nairobi.
He forgot how to talk, only
quoting great passages from books.
He was Basho in skinny jeans and a Samsung tablet
with enough data to send coded letters to his subscribers.
He fell in love with the Chinese winter.

Promenade

Certain truths, you hold them against the light,
and they change color.

I am a cartographer of water. I
walk on it as long as it is an inch deep.

In a sense, I am either the dog,
or the lady with the dog.

The Lights in Zanzibar

You say the idea of collecting shells off the coast of
    Kenya—South Coast—
is a fantasy of an animal looking for its conscience in sand.
You'd like to spend your life near the big lake
but not close enough to hear the lapping of waves against naked
    stone.
Our lives revolve around ambition and a force
like a minister speaking at a funeral wake.

At night, when you walk down the coast at low tide,
you can see the light in Zanzibar.
A string of beads on the seceding land,
receding saltwater.
    At night
you can see the bodies floating in the water, swept up by the
    currents—
the bodies of drowned men clutching their wives' clutch bags—
all the way from Zanzibar.

The reef is an imaginable wall of resistance, put up
by dreams of drowned ferries.
In the paper it said the ferry moaned like a whale. Some salty
    music
before its last dive.
I call you from kilometers away, to ask you about leaving for the
    South Coast
where, if it dark enough, you can see the light in
    Zanzibar.

Eternally Distracted

And I am searching inside the skull head
for bop pop, which I find through earphones
in an impersonal room where
I have dreamed up—in my immersion—a
scene for a black-and-white film
starring starlings and black bodies.
It's the room where my dirty shavings are hidden,
where I am eternally distracted
by the outlines and summaries of books
not the content. Pornography
is a recluse if you can watch the TV set and smile
at anchors and at the same time hold one hand above
the skull head and dream up the god of
the god of distraction. It is not certain
this girl I knew lost her virginity, but
we like to assume she did so
as we were distracted by the light coming in
from the open beaks of robins.
The language of you is icons
supplemented by how letters
can be arranged into images.

Ghostwriter

A Found Poem

(Adult Content) Ghostwriter for Erotic Stories and Paranormal Erotica
Requires 6 hardcore erotic adult content short stories.
Payment will be a total of $150 USD for this project.
    NO incest, rape, or
assault, and all characters must be over 18 years old.
Each short story must be 4500 word minimum, 7000 word maximum.
Each story must be different and a complete story including a
    suggested title for each.
We require good story lines and Explicit XXX content.
The writing must be of a good standard, contemporary and with a
    light touch.
Be very graphic in your descriptions of sex, the smell, the taste, and
    so on . . . it's porn with words.
Stories must be written for heterosexual women and may include
    multiple partners,
threesomes, gangbangs,
bisexual, and lesbian. Explicit sex scenes.
.doc file format.
Also looking for Paranormal erotica stories (Vampire/Werewolf/
    Ghost sex)

Explicit hardcore sexual description and some dirty language
required.
The sex must be couched within a story.
This work takes a special kind of writer, please attach a sample of
    one COMPLETE erotic story you have written.

also with each story we would need a small synopsis or
    description . . . about 100 words.

Obviously, the work must be ORIGINAL and we will check this.
   You agree
that you will own no rights to the work or parts of
the work and you understand/agree your
name will not appear anywhere on the work. We will retain all
   copyrights to any of these stories.

American English writer preferred.

Shakara

Slow dancing to "Shakara,"
I tell you
put me in a room with Fela Kuti, a square room
without windows or doors, like
an infamous childhood riddle for an egg.
Put me in a room with "Shakara,"
I go dance
King David has
nothing on me.
"Shakara" is a silent night near a lake
disturbed only by the cricket soliloquy.
It is an angry Miles Davis in a shiny
leather jacket. I am so many men
when I'm dancing.

Memorial

To the young and able man who lets his death come in
with veils in his face that say you can come in and claim
a place among us. To the young man who closes his eyes
to the parting of clouds and lets what is beyond come in.
To the young man whose body is still warm, that weightless
being with halos, whose footsteps we will never fill. To the
    endless
clock machine in the god body of the young man who
closes his eyes as the light sweeps him to eternity. To the blessed
beating of his heart when we listen to our closed palms.
To the complex latticework of smiles in his photographs
every two seconds you pick him up and back. God body love.
Good-bye. To the young man whose laughter is now a memorial
    among us,
as we sit under tents, listen to our mothers and sisters cry,
shed our own not-so-private god tears love, shelter under
the night that claimed him. To him and beyond and the endless
love through which God privately loves him.

The Nobel Prize for Medicine

I called her number. We talked about Yamanaka and pluripotent
cells. Reversing life and gay men having babies from their
skin cells. But when I mentioned her black stockings, the
ones that come with upholstery, she claimed she did not own
such. Building our life definitions around lab reports and long
nights with assays and gels, that is all I can claim. It is the only
way to be young and in love. That was yesterday. She wins the
night by how dark her vice can be. It is there on her upper lip
like a bridge in mythology. You can look for the aetiology of
words between her legs.

On a Terrace Balcony in Abuja

On a terrace balcony in Abuja, where our screenplays
must not be so obviously poetic, must not
be visual, appraise the body. On a terrace
we sit drinking the national beer
in the only place where there are outdoor air conditioners.
We are poets who must write screenplays
but not so ambiguous as to baffle.

Later, when it is dark and insects are airplanes
around the lighted orbs inside my head,
a young gay man recites Ngugi Wa Thiong'o from memory.
That apostle, great man of my lesser conscientious country.

I tell him I am yet to read Ngugi. I do not
actually say this. I take out my phone,
scroll to my blog, read them some absurdist poem
about a girl who had marigolds growing
from her armpits.
                              After I fucked her there,
                              I left my semen in her reservoir.
They marvel at my cunning, my daring, and offer me
a prostitute. One offers me his stepmother.

We argue about the place of the body in
our work, after we have spent the day leaving bodies
as words on a paper terrace.
Sometimes it rains when the sun is shining,
we feel like strangers on earth.

At night I sob,
marigold
sprouting from my anus.

Algorithm

When searching for the function of orgasms,
the third search result reads:
"Functional MRI of the brain during orgasm in women."
Such is the Google algorithm,
now cruising inside our bodies.

Reality Television

I wish you'd stop telling me to classify "want future sex."
We, as a minor infringement of the law,
we have spent all day sending each other messages
that might be riddles to our consciences, if we had any.
Messages like favorite sexual positions, time of day,
what we ate for lunch (bread, vegetables,
fish, mayonnaise) from a fortnight ago.
As I put down a novel and pick up the *Myth of Sisyphus*,
you are in the other room watching reality T V
about bad girls who live together and drink tequila all day.
I press on through the preface toward absurdity and suicide.

September

Listen to their uninterrupted sirens.
They are the hosts of unsung bodies.
It is September Ten now and there is no sun,
just them, in costume.
Now there is an orchestra
I have no way of getting into,
I'm not invited into my own body.
I like short sentences.
Tomorrow will be September Ten.
I do not play an instrument.
I have to dispose of this host.

This body's sirens:
There is music here.

Principles of Variations

I. THE CURTAINS OUR KISSES

In bed you sought signs of a massacre on my hands.
The morning begins with your
tired fingers finding the sun under the tiles,
some meals we call tender activism,
Sauvignon in paper cups
speaking thick Swahili your mouth a trampoline.
A shipwreck in my blood yearns to be found
as a treasure perfect for your dress.
Floating on your skin
all the words a palate can hold.

> We tremble at night, new leaves
> bud from the sides where limbs
> were cut off, this new light
> emblazons our new skin-hides.
> Your face is a lamina complete
> with a network of tears, holes
> in your palms for the times we
> sacrifice love for poems. Your
> makeup hues adobe walls, I kiss
> the hem of your dress and leave
> you a virgin.

Where the brewing coffee can reach your lips,
each raindrop is a word you learn to remember
with the levees of your sandals
as an act of love.
You blow up the carcass of an umbrella,
and I am glad to offer you a disguise.

In the delicatessen
your palms and eyes
conspire.

The shelves of marble sweets.
My blood under your nails.

A room
where you throw love to me
three times a day.

Otto Gross

You were a man when I was young.
Hard to tell now as you ask me for money
to buy liquor. You introduce me as your young brother.
Here is the scene of our night in Stendikisa:
buses bound to Nairobi at 80 kmph–
we think how our organs would flower
against such contact.
We think of a going away
under the influence as a sort of lazy philosophy
of reparation to God. Such a big and empty word.
atonement is. The night is dark
and I'm thinking of the fast buses approaching,
my penis growing hard as the cement
   of new African superhighways.

Life has turned into an event you see
through aSteadicam.
YouTube aesthetics define us properly.

Oh starry night, the ghost of Otto Gross,
where art thou?

Central Park

Yes, perhaps I write a letter to a neon god
flawed by lashes of those who created it.

Sadness is a park bench, a blackbird's attempt
at organ music.

Where a man, homeless and without traces of footsteps back to
    the center
un-feathers
my blackbird on a park bench for dinner.

First time I buy a Pepsi-Cola, I brood
over a paradise lost in Central Park,
watch strangers make their way to Community
without a glance at the green grass,
a child falling from the swing,
or feeding the pigeons with stale bread crumbs.
On their shoulder blades fairies are finding squares
to light their wings on fire.
But, again (my face almost in the halo
of a disco ball), I sigh,
waiting for darkness. I find one or three songs
to make my own club remix,
I am dancing on pavements,
avenues, lanes, walks, arcades,
imagining skinny girls, nude.
The metropolis is simply a plot.
And who feeds the pigeons?

Over the shoulders of he who shares a park bench,
Tahrir Square on the *Daily Nation.*
I want to whisper *Tahrir* like a lover,
let him know that sometimes I watch the news
and catch glimpses of blood.

Desertion

A friend is
in a hospital bed, narrow cell,
Avenue Hospital, Psychiatric Ward.
Silly drugs go up and down
her capillaries, looking for
unoccupied thought rooms
where the music
has been playing—a sensational
braying for a decade. "I saw
the best mind of my generation
destroyed by madness." She
swallowed industrial paint
and hypochlorite detergent
to cover and clean the inside.
She swallowed the industrial dust
from the graves of her living parents.
She studies the blue sky of day
for signs of a stubborn star.
She looks for roads in the Sahara
where her bones are
hidden roads to desertion.

New House

We have new walls, without paint, new doors that slide without a sound, a new chandelier the bulbs of lilies glowing in there like babies waiting to be born. Observe dimming lights fall on dusty tiles, hold that thread.

My room is a place with its own couch where I sit and listen to the drone of engines as airplanes take off from JKIA, behind the curtains sometimes a bird will get trapped, flutter against the window. The small, red bird will view my attempts to free it as false, like the CAT truck arms of the present regime, so it will continue to flatter until it is out of breath, and the music it will make will never be the same.

Curtains are left drawn to obstruct any attempts of shadows watching me sleep.

I free the bird at last and it will perch on my neighbor's tree. We cut down our new shrubs.

Cousins have moved in and one is a drunkard although I am, too, in secret. He fills the new house with the smell of Sportsman cigarettes, smelling feet, sweat, and finally (maybe this is what it feels like to have a man in the house) urine.

Her blood is a pantoum, but I could just as easily have imagined it.

My brother comes from church with his new deodorant air. My mother has imported perfume in her dresses, and all this gives me headaches. Often I can smell apples through the morning curtains. Often it is a trick of rain. (Remember the thread.)

In the upward well is the white underside of a dead lizard, a recurring Narcissus. Everywhere, lizards darting across the compound, jumping onto walls only to come back when my footsteps are outworn.

Newts like old men hunting for flies in the latrine. Flies have a day to complete their life cycle and I think this a dream.

Also so much space for rats to run in, they eat through underwear like cotton candy.

I spend time in my room watching reruns. I think about the meniscus of my cornea and if I should attempt a self-portrait.

The Anointing

I'd raise my hand in class whenever the catechist asked a
  question,
I always volunteered to read the scriptures.
On the day of the anointing I was moody for some reason
but I remember so much,
I remember that one moment caught in the photograph.

The green couch.
This was once a maroon couch before the
second carpenter's touch.
It must be where my brother was made.
The wood on one side is broken,
the insides full of rat and cockroach dropping.
It sings like a *kayamba.*
The green velvet is where I used to draw lines and rub them,
where I almost broke a girl's virginity
but (she got scared and told me to stop)
where another girl slept,
where another spilled red wine,
where all my friends clustered and talked about our yesterdays,
where I loose my coins, receipts, nail clippings.

I Could Smell Them

For a long time I could see the things they used to mark life with.
The father arrived in a Datsun, the mother had a perpetual
    wedding gown,
tail always dragging behind the monolith or curled up between
    her legs.
I could smell them.
I thought, how graceful they carry bugs in matchboxes.
I longed to mourn a lost one.
They had things. Like analog wristwatches and video games, and
    the children
had hibiscus in their braids,
they dipped tomatoes in warm water and skinned them also.
Was it water or wine in the green bottles? Such a mafia.
I thought about the rain at night and if they ever felt it;
if they were grooming and skinning their young ones.

Lost Stones

Now follow me to lost stones;
all this I beg you.

Collecting dust, offer distractions for
a second, experiencing rain as

stones never to be picked up.
Follow me to the dust. See

how lost some stones can be.

Travel Guide

I pick up a travel guide at your doormat
morning when the city wakes up to rain.

Termites float on the leaves waiting to descend
in tune to your sleeping step your step your step.

It's Not the Same as When You Crush Paper Flowers

It's not the same as when you crush paper flowers.
Like this one time you held my hand and told me,
up there is where the Milky Way is,
we were boys, but that's where our milky way is,
between the palms of our hands, you said,
where my lips walk on the tightrope
and I want red velveteen.

It is too late for linking up.
Should I ever touch you touch you touch you,
I believe it will be
sin.

A Bronze God, or a Letter on Demand

I like to think of your silence as the love letters you will not write
　　me,
as two sax solos from two ages across a stage, learning the
　　languages
of kissing with your eyes closed. I like to think of you as a god
to whom I no longer pray, as a god I aspire to. I like the opening
　　of your joined palms,
which is like an urn where my ashes find a home. The music of
　　your lashes;
the silent way your body wears out mine.
Mostly, I like to think of you at night when a black screen of
　　shining dust shines
from your mines to the edge of my skin, where you are a lamp of
　　flutters.
I remember the spectral lashes—marigold, tamarind, secret thing
　　between your thighs,
of closed kissing eyes. At night, the possibility of you is a heavy
sculpture of heavy bronze at the side of my bed,
a god. And I pray you into life. Into flesh.

Birds

There is a house full of what you might call birds, species never before seen, some thought of as extinct. When I point out a bird by an all-weather road, instead of looking at it you look at me, you say it makes you happy to see me so taken in. I sight the same bird a week later, when you are not with me. I like this skin, that I can always take leave. There is a body full of what you might call birds, and the way I view you as an approaching bird. You must see these walls as containing us, rather than a dark house of forgotten birds. I welcome the birds at the end of the day, when they must question us with their singing. I swear to you, this is no metaphor. The cold means flowers bloom slowly. Flowers from your ears and mouth, like cotton on a dead body. There is dust in my eyes and I'd like you to lick it. There is music in my throat and I'd like you to kiss it. When I see the bird I will be seeing you, I will take you home, get into your skin. Dear young poet, I will repossess my house of birds.

Imitation Bodies

Yet, I talk to you as is the fashion
of the forewords of books by unknown authors.

Imitation bodies.

Eyes, an unblinking display, closed signals
of a time we used to talk, exploding into vowels and vapor,

fingers stretching out, collapsible on contact with light.
We were magnificent, living dead along a vertical bed.

Now I decode teleprompts in the eyes of strangers
as private, momentary thoughts we had.

Walking along a street I meet you from another time,
almost holding the hand of the other, lover.

You do not see me,
but our reflections quiver on the walls of banking halls, signals

ferrying our souls to the park, the café, or, alas, back home
alone to a pile of laundry, mothballs, books, dolls.

For now, you balance on flat heels,
contemplating new and emerging markets for

the experiments we call dreams.
You forget when we invented a different language

to be broadcast through touch.
Its etymology was a thing hidden in the future.

Our eyes are now coated
in the mascara of strangers;

a film of gold
paves our vision as soon as a blink is possible.

The languages we are busy forgetting
is our only accomplice.

We are all strangers in this city,
existential sheep in traffic.

My Sisters Used to Put Me in Dresses

My sisters used to put me in dresses,
mascara and red heels;
a green leather bag and red beads.
I was their Christmas pine.
They would make merry,
take Polaroid pictures
as I swirled between old furniture,
and shove me around their bedroom.
I was eight then.
Yesterday, on my twenty-third birthday
they walked into my room
to see me in a red dress
striking poses, smoking Embassy.
None of them laughed.
None wants to stare at the whiteness
of the pearls in my eyes.

Unclaimed

She handles me the same way
the Kenya Police handles crime scene evidence,
all the bodies thrown
   into black body bags.

I am distracted by things such as
where unclaimed bodies are taken. When
you touch me at night I think of mass graves in Benghazi.
I saw in Al Jazeera;
the Spring has found its way to
the wire springs under my bed.

Mountain

On the day I set out on the climb,
grief saddled in my back like a bag of marbles,
my breath like clouds hanging on the low peaks of a mountain,
on the day I set out
leaving nothing behind, nothing on the bed, no version of myself,
just my voice through the night, the voice I use to ward off
    nightmares.
(My voice is a still life in itself, a shroud green and ultramarine
    deep blue,
a bowl of apples and tangerines on a table.)
On the day I set out,
the mountain is high in front of me, the unreliable god of mist
    and fog.
I have no voice to say how high
my fingers must lift as if on a lover's upper lip,
to take in the breath of how high my mountain is—white teeth
    behind
a snow cap, numberless springs, cold like the enzymes in spit—
a version of me is still asleep: the moving of a limb in sleep.
Everything becomes lucid.

Strange Male

You are mad at the happy people in advertisement.
I am mad at news anchors who do not
look me straight in the eyes during prime time news.

You are my sweet limousine on a lease.
Those unclaimed bodies in mass graves,
do they elbow each other for a little more space,
fight over the blanket of soil above
a little extra warmth?

Are their mercies, reprisals, and eternal lives
unclaimed;
The tortured afterlife unclaimed?

A cook show host on channel 52—
she's pregnant. I confess to you,
pregnant women turn me on.

You say: pregnant rats will miscarry if
approached by the scented ghost of a strange male.

Merchant of Flesh

In the morning after the night you lost your virginity,
we sit in bed. I'm thinking about smoking.
It has been raining all night and the dripping water stirs on my
    left lung.
You say: "I'll take a pound of your flesh," and
we spend the morning arguing if I should use the phrase
in a poem.
   Finally, you confess: "I read it in the *Merchant of Venice.*"

There is a stirring in your body,
like what the malaria parasite can do to a pound of flesh.

Playhouse Lane

Shoes outside the big mosque, beads on sale, down to the last call
of the muezzin.
I like it when the sun is hiding and bodies move in closer, a
narrow street is not enough,
veiled ladies sell the seeds of *mbuyu* laced with a hint of pepper
for ten shillings
behind the place with two lions, chains on the gate, like
sculptures could ever bite
a new Turkish restaurant, new in the sense that its linoleum is
ever clean,
the smiles on attendants ever full, a terrace where it must be cool
to smoke.
Color plans on big advertisements have replaced the gray of
buildings.
Ghosts must play behind sealed-off parking lots where a building
burnt down.
We still breathe in the ashes, remember the dead, and demolish
what is left.
A short lane of potted plants, a bar where the smoke from last
night can reach you,
hiding outdoor seats where time sneaks up on lovers.
On the painted glass you can see trapped images of dancers from
last night,
lost in embraces and near long kisses, in Bill Kahora's *Urban
Zoning* where there is no morning.
A faint shower from a leaking pipe, twenty floors up, cold
morning.
The statue of a leader, the offices of a leader, the street named after
a leader:
beware of con-artists posing as insurance sales agents, as leaders.

Bodies, more bodies, traffic lights, more narrow streets which
    beautiful women must avoid;
penumbras where smoking zones should be, ersatz gazebo,
    meditation lane,
a steeple if you are lucky, a basilica where at 2 a.m. you can buy
a rosary and have her tie it around your neck, with cold fingers.
    Next to a casino,
there is another old statue which we have come to forget.
A clean street, a grave, a clock, a fountain, black-white
    pavements,
a dirty street, the government press, a building where she works,
    a clock
where once you stood watching her in a short skirt and black
    stockings.
She found Jesus, she has no time for talking. Her blue eyes are the
    blue of banking halls.
Movie posters advertise pulp fiction. You can get film noir if you
    order early
and inside, rich men we have come to suspect, sip coffee from
    small cups, their white *kanzus*,
the white of mosque tiles, where the call of the muezzin
    announces prayer time.

Let Us Now Talk about Your Waist, Saying

Let us now talk about your waist, saying,
every part of you begins with music
and ends with a reconciliation of man with God.
The rhinestone waist, porcelain, crushed flowers, hallucinogens,
my steps, grinding. My tongue. Your waist, a valediction
are we now dancing to Arabic drums? No.
It is a long silence, your waist. Anodyne.
It is reading a letter written across time.
I write to my younger self and you are with me burning the letter.
"Take risks, hold my waist," you say. "Take me inside your mouth
where my Rilke and Anne Sexton and Federico Lorca live."
You allow me to misspell adjectives there, you
let my tongue take in heavy verbs and offer rolled adverbs
from the conceptualists to jazz improvisation. You are breaking
the wave of my tongue on your tongue when you laugh.
Is it possible to come inside my mouth
with your hair held back in pins? I could plagiarize you
from the black tombstone where your waist was shaped,
I must not digress from your waist.
Ah, life is your waist, circumspect, that quiet dancing when I'm
    going down on you.

Dancers

When Brahem Anouar and Dave Holland play,
I see two dancers, one taking the lead, the other
watching, removed from the stage, giving
his partner time. Then she joins in.

I tell her this,
"Love is the body of an elephant's tail,
leave the rest to God."

A Benzedrine Hallucination

Keeping my pan-Africanism, or lack thereof, in check
not reading Negritude,
hiding in my room. I read Kerouac, embarrassed.
Sucking at my thumb, I come to these people
as I have come into everything in my life,
with no inhibitions except the fear
that I know they speak of inhibitions.

Madman at Kilifi

Gossamer in her eyes, my eyes.
We see algae on the walls on the small of her back.

He wears polythene bags around his girth, a
lost superhero of my lost childhood.
He means no harm. At the
intersection of a bank and wholesale shop he sits
contemplating the lovers
he sees walking, mad at each other.
I am lover, she is lover.
He looks like the animation on a Michelin ad, I say.

At night, when the town is asleep,
We explore the Swahili architecture of the new building,
How it humbly subscribes to modernity.
We consider
running up the stairs to the rooftop swimming pool
to swim naked.

But no,
we eat at Kuku Ali's,
who roasts chicken under a half moon.

We walk past the bridge,
the Indian Ocean is a small estuary under our green exuberant
    toes.

At night.
My God, at night.

We investigate
the various levels of your vagina, score music
on replay, a Jamaican jam.

My God.

The gauze on your window is broken
letting in insects that beat against our skin.
See, nature does not hide. Nature
seeks to join.

My tongue seeks the scent of blooming mango flowers
inside your ears.

Young

There was a time we needed to experiment
with drugs and jazz records, hallucinogens
and men, a long time ago.

We wanted nothing but men, to reclaim
them like land buried under sea.

We thought it was a fun thing to have
gay friends and hang out in gay bars:
pretend cigarettes were phalli.

That was when we were young,
psychoanalysts of water and land.

Reclaiming a Beloved City

I approach Nairobi, thrown into the mass of old avenues. I have a map of the old town and what the streets used to be called, government road and the little place where Lord Delamere liked to be the asshole, all regards to the dead.

And in the eyes of people are azaleas blooming and popping like bubblegum carried up to perch in the branches of a blue I&M tree, there where the transmission has been telling us consumption begins and ends when our bodies decide. We are lapping against each other, our bodies not touching, our intentions quite clear, our beds unmade.

A naiad, completely given up to sighs and biting its fingernails, winks at me. I am the inconsolable. She gives me back a second of my celebratory youth.

I am not approached by beggars although to feel at home my eyes beg for some reprieve from the eyes of another traveler who has misplaced his airplane in the middle of the street where it is okay to hold the arms of a stranger until you have crossed the road.

In the old streets I besiege a man to translate the poems on the walls, on the bodies of women, on the lumps that are hanging from their men. Gross desire is a river tapestry with water like ribbons—he tells me.

The Ante-Chamber

In a city with flickering lights,
the wicker more in your eyes than mine,
and boundaries are drawn on the walls,
like memories that never furnish what we call the conscious.

This room can be the ante-chamber if we decide
that this is the body of a father whose decay smells
like an old clock rusting away in the ceiling.

Beside this father is an encyclopedia,
which is my way of saying "a mistress,"
with her arms and hem around him.

In this room, fear is my immutable bond to boundaries
on their bodies. The portrait
of the mistress heads toward me
where I am the room, the Rex, the paperweight
on his agony.

Imagine Those Slender Cigarettes

Since I read that special Mothers' Day feature in the *Daily Nation,*
about how these street mothers live behind the Sarova Panafric just
    when the city
has gone to bed and only poets and other criminals are awake, I have
    imagined
slender fingers, holding cheap lighters up, fiends cheering.
There is a hierarchy of who draws the longest, depending on the
    trimester.
    As the cigarette smoke mixes with the progesterone,
the night is ablaze with evolving nova. If only the roof could bother
    them to see it.
Such things as the evolution of nova (God's own simple pleasures)
cannot precede the need for shelter.
The universe, if it so pleases, can multiply *in utero*. Imagine those
    slender cigarettes
of their Casablanca nights, metronomes.
Out of nowhere a cop shows up, not to arrest or rape them, no,
much worse—he quotes the new constitution.

Concerto of the Unconcerned

Our New Wave group, Concerto of the Unconcerned,
has taken to painting roads with gray graffiti,
jump walls to the buildings and maelstrom inside,
and take videos of their copulating with tambourines,
second cousins, strangers. Our photographs and other marginalia
are the hazard of passive protest.
This is the way we have sex
with our New Wave pocket dictionaries, eyes shut.
Where has the revolution taken us, dirty lovers?
These are our new poems of unbecoming
budding from the spray can images of a dreamy Lorca.

Galilee

Did you wake up today beside your favorite alibi?
Picture this:
a tent in Galilee, silver coins, yellow flowers,
radioactive glows, nuclear power, sins.

Picture this:
a holiday home, a villa overlooking the ocean,
Benguela current,
a night out with Puntland pirates,
binoculars settled on the members of fishermen,
harmlessly.

Picture this:
Bob Marley songs.

A Genre of Isolation

The great revolt of night
against the sum of my homosexual tendencies:
rage.

A ritual dichotomy of limbs
your body needs to forget;
Dream-catching my voice between your thighs.

Salt
on the window pane.
You teach me how to lick memory.

Bride

My bride says there is something in the shadows.
I believe I can see a material salt pillar,
a mirror in her words, my bride.
The veil in front of her face is a swinging bridge,
and if she says
there is something in the shadows
I believe.
I am something—my opalescent tears tell me I'm something.
My vessel bride is in the shadows.
A veil flutters out of the open window.
her dress is a communal shadow.
I watch as she reads her prescriptions,
as she goes mad.

Treason

Under a bridge flows the residue
of our treasons.
That blue Saturday,
the sun casts figures in the water
of the blue estuary.

Cucu Njeri

An ancient Galapagos bird,
Cucu Njeri, carried her children in a basket
into a 6x5 apartment
   in Korogocho
where pit latrines smelled of gargoyle breath.
Not strictly "apartment," more like—
well, Cucu Njeri weaved a web,
trapped us in temporary places,
although her daughters' limbs were free to part . . .
More like that, as I said.
She breathed life into the daughters of Mumbi;
four daughters, four rubies in the bush,
four rupees in the city; odd jobs, laughter, Rexona, bread.
Nonetheless, Cucu breathed her mighty air
into trunks of skin.
Ha! An apartment
   in Golgotha.

I still mean to place chrysanthemums on your grave,
red soil in Lang'ata Cemetery.
I still do. I still want to cry, remember you, Cucu.
Once again you will cradle
me in the soil of your palms, with arms of decay,
and make it easy for me.

I know you will understand the absence of tears.
I still mean to look for the headstone
with your name,
and place on it an impression of chrysanthemums.

The Latrine of Giardia

The latrine of Giardia rots
like atheists' beliefs, government condoms, and long-
forgotten babies.
I have a love for deep, frothing black-green of latrines
larva-sweet like gravy from a lover's lips; weevils in my *githeri*
Buya! One man selecta!
I want latrines
so dirty you have to squat around the periphery:
You, you, you. Let he who does not shit cast the first stone.
Aren't we building our own tower of Babel?
Eh! Shit drops into the puddle in different tongues,
I tell you, my man.
When I was this young I saw a madman's shit.
It is only then I understood
that my nation is anointed in oily stool.

A turbaned *mokorino* saunters through and through
burning tires, hailing *"Cabbeshi, Cabbeshi Mbao!"*
I hear
"Hail the Messiah, Hail the Messiah."
He is the only one mad enough to sell
tarred shells of smiling corollas, long dead.
Also, he rides his own, I say, his own cart.
And he wears a turban.

I was surprised to have been baptized Antonio,
but when Father Mario said
"Anthony. Anthony with an H, *nakubatiza*
Kwa jina la Baba . . . "
I saw it best to take the name.
Anyway, it was Susan's idea to name me Antonio.

If it were up to me they'd call me
St. Augustine of Hippo, or, Bonaparte, Gama pinto.
Wait, I got it now. How about Nkrunziza?
Of course I had no idea
who the Augustine or partying fellaz were,
but words like *Confession* and *Josephine* always allured me.
Also, Master Augustine sounds
way better than Master Antonio,
which always makes me want to do the chicken dance.
I'm Anthony, by the way, son of Susan.
And you are?

The Bin

The bin slid into our lives like a slow, benign
hereditary madness, Creutzfeldt-Jakobs, I shall name it,
which is more original than Kalashnikov.
The site of it, preempted by the stench,
8 a.m's rays on torn PVC and fish baskets,
a white dog with a black eye.
No one but the kids got close to it,
not even Nairobi Bins.
It was a secret cemetery for premature fetuses
and feces neatly wrapped in fascists' old newspapers.
Sorting through the residues of my predecessors,
it was the happiest time of my life,
the bin, 1800hrs,
it was only The Tank of Colossal Power,
inspired by Jamhuri Day celebrations.
The Old Cannon sent fireballs into the night
Poosh! Voosh! Die Father. Silently. Please.
A happy life meant blaming the ones who came before us.
Where have you been, Nairobi?

A sketch of the dark: headlights of cars disappearing
into the bushes, the dark-purple outline
of hills, like hoods.
Victoria lies in her prehistoric groin
of warm earth.
The moon, lonely, sad, sends its light
to delicately illuminate the daisies.
Such a halo.
Headlights scatter into the dark
like rats into kitchen cabinets.

"Metrosexual"

He wore a dress,
walked among the shells
he had gathered,
made necklaces,
and with another
sired a daughter.

Approaching Siaya

A place of many shores,
a cloud of dusk on the lake:
rain.
Islands of soft tissue in the wake,
a muddy procession to a funeral.

I will not say good-bye this way:
you with your perfect make-up,
a veil on your face,
and me with mud in my shoes,
in the company of past lovers
lowering your coffin,
waiting for our good-bye.

IN THE AFRICAN POETRY BOOK SERIES

The Promise of Hope:
New and Selected Poems, 1964–2013
Kofi Awoonor
Edited and with an introduction
by Kofi Anyidoho

Madman at Kilifi
Clifton Gachagua

Seven New Generation African Poets:
A Chapbook boxed set
Edited by Kwame Dawes
and Chris Abani

To order or obtain more information on
these or other University of Nebraska
Press titles, visit nebraskapress.unl.edu.

CPSIA information can be obtained at www.ICGtesting.com
Printed in the USA
BVOW03s0346090114

341272BV00003B/6/P